GRIEF RECOVERY

A Workbook for Widows and Widowers

Revised Edition

Robyn Ledwith Mar

THERE IS HOPE
YOU CAN RECOVER
YOU WILL SURVIVE AND LIVE AGAIN

Blessed are they who mourn, for they shall be comforted.
Matthew 5: 4 (NIV)

authorHOUSE®

AuthorHouse™
1663 Liberty Drive
Bloomington, IN 47403
www.authorhouse.com
Phone: 833-262-8899

Published by AuthorHouse 04/13/2022

ISBN: 978-1-6655-3858-9 (sc)
ISBN: 978-1-6655-3857-2 (e)

Print information available on the last page.

Any people depicted in stock imagery provided by Getty Images are models, and such images are being used for illustrative purposes only. Certain stock imagery © Getty Images.

This book is printed on acid-free paper.

Because of the dynamic nature of the Internet, any web addresses or links contained in this book may have changed since publication and may no longer be valid. The views expressed in this work are solely those of the author and do not necessarily reflect the views of the publisher, and the publisher hereby disclaims any responsibility for them.

Scripture quotations marked NIV are taken from the Holy Bible, New International Version®. NIV®. Copyright © 1973, 1978, 1984 by International Bible Society. Used by permission of Zondervan. All rights reserved. [Biblica]

Scripture quotations marked NKJV are taken from the New King James Version. Copyright © 1982 by Thomas Nelson, Inc. Used by permission. All rights reserved.

Scripture quotations marked NASB are taken from the New American Standard Bible®, Copyright © 1960, 1962, 1963, 1968, 1971, 1972, 1973, 1975, 1977, 1995 by The Lockman Foundation. Used by permission.

I would like to thank Merrilee Harter Mitchell for her dedication to this ministry and her invaluable assistance in revising this updated edition.

Contents

Contents

GRIEF RECOVERY

Introduction

This workbook was originally written for the Menlo Park Presbyterian Church Widows and Widowers Support Group of Menlo Park, California. It was designed to provide structure for members of a support group so that issues associated with grieving could be better understood and recovery from the pain of grief could be accelerated.

The purpose of this support group was to provide a safe place for widows and widowers to express their emotions, to share their experiences of deep grief, to understand their grief journey, and to help them look forward to new lives. The fact that it was not a professional therapy group seemed to give the group members a greater sense of freedom in opening their lives to one another. Through the discussion and sharing, those in the group were able to find comfort and begin their recovery.

The premise of the workbook is that we can recover from the pain of grief. After the death of my husband in 1983, when I was 56 years old, I began my own journey toward recovery. Through this time, God brought me back to Himself and into the family of His church. He provided friends who listened and cared, and prayer partners who helped me work through the grief.

In 1990 I was asked by my pastor to start a Grief Support Group for Widows and Widowers at the church. I did research, read books, and took notes. The result was the first workbook which was written in 1993, printed, used in groups, and formally published by AuthorHouse in 2010. The purpose of this revision is to bring the book up to date with some changes in current thinking about the journey through grief.

My experiences with sharing in support groups have convinced me that this is the heart of recovery. It is gratifying to see the progress that group members make in even 10 weeks, and if they continue to use the workbook as their companion on their grief journey, it will be exciting to see the changes in their lives.

The death of a spouse is one of the most difficult things we will ever experience. It is physically, emotionally, and spiritually exhausting. The bereaved feel lost, traumatized, and stunned. But with God's help and the support of others who understand the pain, those who have losses can be given the hope that they will recover. I believe that together they can work through the grieving process and will not only survive, but fully live again.

The best description of this support program can be found at the end of the workbook: *How to Start and Lead a Widows and Widowers Ministry at Your Church.*

Robyn Ledwith Mar
2021

GRIEF RECOVERY

Scripture

Turn to me and be gracious to me, for I am lonely and afflicted.
The troubles of my heart have multiplied; free me from my anguish.
Look upon my affliction and my distress and take away all my sins.
Psalm 25: 16-18 (NIV)

"For I know the plans I have for you," declares the Lord, "plans to prosper you
and not to harm you, plans to give you hope and a future."
Jeremiah 29: 11 (NIV)

"For my thoughts are not your thoughts, neither are your ways my ways,"
declares the Lord.
"As the heavens are higher than the earth, so are my ways higher than your ways and
my thoughts than your thoughts."
Isaiah 55: 8-9 (NIV)

Then Job replied to the Lord:
"I know that you can do all things; no purpose of yours can be thwarted.
You asked 'Who is this that obscures my plans without knowledge?'
Surely, I spoke of things I did not understand,
things too wonderful for me to know."
Job 42: 1-3 (NIV)

And we know that in all things God works for the good of those who love him,
who have been called according to his purpose.
Romans 8: 28 (NIV)

"I am the resurrection and the life.
The one who believes in me will live, even though they die;
and whoever lives by believing in me will never die."
John 11: 25 (NIV)

Do not be anxious about anything, but in everything, by prayer and petition, with
thanksgiving, present your requests to God. And the peace of God, which transcends
all understanding, will guard your hearts and your minds in Christ Jesus.
Philippians 4: 6-7 (NIV)

GRIEF RECOVERY

THERE IS HOPE
YOU CAN RECOVER
YOU WILL SURVIVE AND LIVE AGAIN

Even though I walk through the valley of the shadow of death,
I will fear no evil, for you are with me; your rod and your staff they comfort me.
Psalm 23: 4 (NIV)

Week 1 The Loss - Numbness and Shock

Initially after our loss we are in a state of shock. Whether the death has been anticipated or is unexpected, we find that we are disoriented, frightened and confused. We can't grasp what has happened. Our world has stopped. There seems to be no future, only blackness and emptiness.

"The last time I saw Ted, he was going out the door to work. I was busy with the children and didn't take the time to give him a kiss goodbye. He tried to call me during the day, but I never got back to him. I never dreamed that I would never see him again. I'll never forget the call from the police, telling me that he had collapsed on the way home. I just can't believe that he's gone. I never had the chance to tell him goodbye."

"We knew that Marian's cancer was spreading and that there wasn't too much hope. Yet we continued to pray and plan for a future. I was so certain that God would heal her. Why did He let her die? I can't stop thinking about it."

"John had such a long illness that we were able to prepare for his death. He had planned everything for me, and seemed to be at peace. I thought that I was ready to let him go. I had no idea that it would be so hard. I just can't seem to stop crying. I can't do the simplest things. I don't think I'll ever recover."

"When I got out of the car at the cemetery my legs buckled and I had to be half-carried to the gravesite."

How we feel

Even though we may feel numb, underneath there is terrible pain. We know that we must get through the first few days of our loss, so we refuse to feel the pain. We may be so turned inward that we are unaware of what we are doing. We may be trying so hard to control our emotions that we deny ourselves the comfort of tears. It is important that we give ourselves permission to feel the loss, to grieve, to cry out.

How we react to our grief

While grieving we may not be able to pay attention to everyday matters. It may seem that we are out of touch with reality. Our minds are in a state of emergency, similar to the body's reaction to a major wound. We may not hear what others say to us or respond coherently. We may initially be able to cope and seem efficient, only to collapse a few days later.

Some common reactions during the first weeks of loss are:

Disbelief - a sense of unreality: we can't believe what has happened.

Sudden or constant crying and sobbing

Feeling numb, confused, or disoriented

Sleeplessness or unusual sleep patterns

Physical pain or illness

Periods of extreme anxiety

A sense of isolation

Becoming hyperactively busy or being unable to concentrate at work

Momentarily forgetting that the loss has occurred

Overwhelmed by memories

Fear of the future and/or financial insecurity

How to help ourselves:

It is very important that we take care of ourselves, both physically and emotionally:

Ask for practical help from friends and relatives

Don't be hard on yourself - don't expect too much

Allow yourself to mourn: you don't have to be brave

Help your children deal with the loss

Find responsive friends who can and will listen to you

Let others express their grief to you

Be honest about your grieving

Don't worry that you are "burdening" your friends

Your decision: To recognize that you have suffered loss, are in deep grief, and need help.

Questions:

1. On a separate sheet of paper, describe as fully as you can the circumstances of your spouse's death. This may be the start of journaling, or writing down your feelings. Many people find it extremely helpful during the recovery process. (See the Notes and Journaling pages at the back of this workbook.)

2. Describe your physical reactions at the time of loss.

3. Have you been able to talk to someone about how you feel? Who? When?

4. Have your family and friends been helpful to you? If so, in what way?

Personal prayer at home:
Tell God about your pain and how much you hurt. Ask for His comforting arms to support you. Our God understands grief. Jesus wept when he saw how Mary and Martha were grieving the death of their brother, Lazarus.

GRIEF RECOVERY

THERE IS HOPE
YOU CAN RECOVER
YOU WILL SURVIVE AND LIVE AGAIN

"A time is coming and has come when you will be scattered, each to your own home. You will leave me all alone. Yet I am not alone, for my Father is with me. I have told you these things, so that in me you may have peace. In this world you will have trouble. But take heart! I have overcome the world." John 16: 32-33 (NIV)

Week 2   Facing Our Loss

In the midst of grief, we have difficulty in knowing how to cope. We are torn by emotion and can't find a solid foundation for our feet. We reach back into our past and find little or no experience to help us with the present. Our relatives and friends don't seem to know what to say - and at times their attempts to comfort us are not helpful. We feel awkward and don't know how to express our grief except by emotional outburst or silence. Why don't we know how to deal with our loss?

> "I remember feeling like the front half of me had been ripped off and I had all these sharp shards that hurt anytime they were emotionally touched – by a word, a memory, or an action that brought the loss to the front and center of my mind; then tears flowed."

How we didn't learn how to grieve as children

Some of us were fortunate and grew up in loving and expressive families where the deaths of our relatives and friends were accepted and mourned. But many of us were conditioned as children not to express our grief. As children we might have learned that we must deny our feelings or that it was somehow improper to show grief.

As adults we are now faced with an overwhelming loss. How can we learn to accept our grief and acknowledge our feelings? We must try to understand our emotions and be honest with ourselves about how we feel. As grieving adults (and grieving children, too) we must:

    Learn to express, not to repress, our feelings

    Accept that our loss cannot be replaced

    Accept others' help in grieving

    Understand that it will take time to recover

    Try not to have regrets about the past - we did the best we could

How others view us

Not only ourselves, but others don't know how to deal with loss. They are embarrassed by our grief. Often, they don't know what to say or they try to encourage us to act as though we have already recovered. They want their help to be effective, but don't always know how to be helpful:

> They are afraid of our emotions - it is threatening to them
> They don't want to talk about it - death and loss are uncomfortable subjects
> They want us to be brave - our emotions are difficult for them to handle
> They expect us to recover quickly: "you really should be feeling better by now"
> They think that if we keep busy it will help us

The Academy Award Recovery

Sometimes we are so successful at convincing others that we are "OK" that we appear to achieve an amazing recovery. Our performance is worthy of an Academy Award. We want the approval of others, so we put a smile on our faces and pretend that everything is OK. The effort involved in stuffing our emotions and pretending that we are doing better than we are is not good for us and can lead to behavioral disorders such as over-medication, alcohol abuse, or eating problems. It is important that we not put on a good show to please others or meet their expectations about our recovery. We are unique individuals and should deal with our grief at our own pace and in our own way.

What if we are angry with God?

Our faith may be shaken at this time. We may feel that God has not answered our prayers in allowing our loved one to die, and anger at God can be a normal response to the death of a loved one. Our friends and relatives may be concerned if we question our faith, but we have to be able to work through any anger with God and not be judged for it. Sometimes people give up on their faith because they weren't able to resolve their feelings of anger. If this happens the griever is cut off from the most powerful support resource he or she has, which is the power of prayer.

What can we do if we are angry with God? First, you can boldly go to God and tell Him that you are angry without feeling guilty about it. Ask for His help as you search the Scriptures for His promises to us and look for the examples that He has given us in the Bible. Many people in the Bible were angry with God, but He answered them, even though the answers weren't always easy. And then continue to pray about it. Ask God to help you through the grieving process, knowing that we can count on His unfailing love to help us overcome our grief.

Your decision: To let yourself be honest about your feelings.

Questions:

1. What did you learn as a child regarding reaction to loss? How did your family cope with death?

2. Have people made inappropriate remarks to you regarding the death of your spouse? List these remarks.

3. What did you say to them? What would be a good way to reply?

4. Have you been giving an "Academy Award" performance? Be specific. Where? With whom? How often? How did it make you feel?

Personal prayer at home:

Tell God about your anger and how unfair life can be. Ask Him to help you deal with your anger in a constructive way.

GRIEF RECOVERY

THERE IS HOPE
YOU CAN RECOVER
YOU WILL SURVIVE AND LIVE AGAIN

Behold, I stand at the door and knock; if any one hears My voice and opens the door, I will come in to him, and will dine with him, and he with Me. Revelation 3: 20 (NASB)

Week 3   When the Grief Returns

When the first shock and numbness have passed there is a time when we are running on pure energy. We take care of practical matters: lawyers, business matters, and immediate problems. We have been doing well, thinking, "This isn't so bad." But then, when the initial crisis has passed and we think that we may be returning to normal, the full realization of what has happened hits us. We see an empty future before us; life has become futile and meaningless. Nothing seems to matter.

> "I thought I was doing so well. Everyone said that I was getting back to normal, whatever that is! I don't understand how depressed I have become; it's like I've gone back to the beginning. The pain is as great as when my husband died. Will it ever get better?"

As this second wave of grief occurs, we may experience some new feelings and emotions. A new realization of the extent of our loss may overwhelm us. It is as though, when the first shock wears off, we are now able to feel the full impact of reality. This is not a dream. We cannot go back. We may suddenly perceive that:

We no longer know who we are; we have lost our sense of identity

Our life has irrevocably changed and will continue to change

We've lost our ability to cope with ordinary things

We are trying to be super busy and it's not working

Our family relationships have become strained

We are still angry about the loss

We are increasingly depressed

We are impatient with others and the world at large

We may have slipped into destructive behavior with alcohol, drugs, or eating disorders.

How we can help ourselves:

It is important to understand that we are grieving for much more than our spouse - we have lost much of our lives and how we are used to living. We are beginning to understand that we will have to build a new world and a new life.

9

We need to recognize what we can do to make ourselves feel better:

> Slow down - mourning is hard work. It requires much attention and enormous energy
>
> Eat sensibly and moderately
>
> Take as much time off from responsibilities as possible
>
> Maintain healthy living habits: physical exercise, get enough rest, relax
>
> Give yourself permission to struggle, to grieve, and to feel bad
>
> Express your emotions at appropriate times without embarrassment
>
> Seek the companionship of those who love you, to talk and to listen

What do we need to do? We must:

> Make the decision to work through the suffering and grief to our new life
>
> Choose to fight rather than to take flight, to deal with circumstances rather than denying them.
>
> To start to make changes in our lives.
>
> Abide in our faith and trust God - to know that He is in control of all things.

Your decision: To begin to understand where you are in the grieving process

Questions:

1. Have you experienced this second wave of grief? When? How did you feel? Are you there now?

2. Are you feeling better, or do you still feel hopeless? Are you anxious about the future?

3. What are some of the things you could do to feel better?

4. Do you feel that God has deserted you?

5. Who has been the most support for you? In what way?

Personal prayer at home:

If you are in the midst of this second wave of grief, tell God about the blackness of your life and ask Him to bring light and comfort to you.

GRIEF RECOVERY

THERE IS HOPE
YOU CAN RECOVER
YOU WILL SURVIVE AND LIVE AGAIN

The Lord is my strength and song, And He has become my salvation.
Psalm 118: 14 (NKJV)

Week 4   The Journey Through Grief

There is no "correct" way to grieve. The grieving process is highly individualized. Although there are recognized reactions to our grieving, not everyone goes through them and there is no set order. It is a fluid process with much overlapping of feelings and emotions. The grieving process is the God-given gift of slowly allowing ourselves to accept what has happened; hence some of the numbness until we are ready to move forward.

How long will it take to recover from the pain of grief?

The grieving process following the loss of a spouse normally takes from two, three or more years. Some people are able to move forward more quickly, sometimes grieving can go on for many years, although this may be the result of not initially dealing with the grief. There is no yardstick to measure progress, only your own sense of relief with the easing of the pain of grief. We will always remember our spouses and the role they played in our own lives.

Why is the length of time to grieve so different for each of us? It can depend on:

Your personality and your way of responding to painful events

How soon you are willing to face your grieving

The length and characteristics of your relationship

How dependent you were upon your spouse for your life's structure and meaning

Whether the loss was sudden or foreseen:

> A death preceded by a long illness may seem to give additional time to prepare for the loss. However, a lengthy illness does not always prepare the survivor for the loss and the strain of caring for the spouse may leave him or her even more vulnerable to stress. This is especially true if the survivor has been the major caregiver during that time.

The kind of support given by family and friends

Prior losses and whether or not they have been fully mourned

Whether a person has ambivalent feelings about the loss:

> Sometimes there have been problems in the marriage or the surviving spouse may even be glad that the long illness is over and that they are now free to get on with life. These seemingly inappropriate feelings can cause even more pain or feelings of guilt.

The social, economic, and personal circumstances in which the individuals must do their grieving, for example, financial problems, poor health, other issues.

Our social conditioning:

> Men and women often respond to a loss in different ways. A woman may be more inclined to display her grief to others, to reach out to people around her, and to talk more openly about the loss. Men are often more inclined to keep their grief to themselves, work hard to avoid losing control in front of others, and refrain from asking for help or assistance. Many men will appear to get on with life and quickly involve themselves in work, and therefore frequently do not recover from grief as well as women, who are more willing to seek help for recovery.

Understanding our personal journey through grief

Those of you who walked through the dying process with your spouse might remember hearing about Elisabeth Kubler-Ross's "Five Stages of Grief" from her influential book **On Death and Dying.** You might even have experienced those stages with your spouse. However, Dr. Kubler-Ross was describing the experience of dying patients, not the grieving by spouses, family and friends after the death. Her work laid the foundation for eventually recognizing that grieving people move through a seemingly chaotic series of intense emotions that is unique to each person. It is a journey that can lead to healing the pain of grief while not forgetting our loved one.

This workbook and group were designed to help you navigate your personal grief journey – one that will continue after this group has finished meeting. Up until this week, we have focused on the *past,* the exercises were designed to remind you of what you may have already experienced and to help you recognize how your family and childhood may have shaped how you grieve.

For the next four weeks, we are looking at issues and tasks appropriate for the *present*. You may have come out of the initial fog and by using this workbook and/or attending this group, you are taking steps to move forward, ready to do the exercises to resolve issues that might be roadblocks affecting your ability to complete this current journey of grief.

During the last three weeks, we will be focusing on the *future* – what you want it to look like and how to get there. We hope that doing these exercises increases your fortitude to stay on course toward the transformation made possible as you heal from the pain of grief. You may not be able to complete some of these exercises; however, we hope you will continue to use this workbook in the future to help you complete this journey. These exercises can also be good discussion topics if your group has reunions periodically after you finish the course.

Trying to avoid grief doesn't work, nor does it work to try to speed through the journey - it will come back later at an inappropriate time. As we have discovered, it takes a lot of courage to allow natural healing to occur. You will discover that there are many natural grief reactions that come in waves with varying degrees of intensity. (See **Common Grief Reactions** on page 41). Your set of grief reactions is unique to you, what is common with others is the emotional "roller coaster" of ups and downs over the course of your journey. Our goal is to help you identify the path of your own journey and reach the point where the pain of grief has lessened substantially and memories bring more smiles than tears, more joy than sorrow.

Your decision: Will you trust God to help you move on through your grief journey?

Questions:

1. Are you able to recognize the grief reactions you have already experienced?

2. Where do you think you are now on your journey of grief?

Date of Death   A New Future

_____

3. Does your grieving seem hopeless to you, or are you able to have hope?

4. Is understanding more about your personal grief journey helpful to you? In what way?

Personal prayer at home:

Ask God to give you the faith to trust Him as you move through this painful time.

THERE IS HOPE
YOU CAN RECOVER
YOU WILL SURVIVE AND LIVE AGAIN

And surely, I am with you always, even to the end of the age. Matthew 28: 20 (NIV)
Just as I have been with Moses, I will be with you; I will not fail you or forsake you.
Joshua 1: 5 (NIV)

Week 5   Choosing to Recover from the Pain of Grief

Some time later, Jesus went up to Jerusalem for a feast of the Jews. Now there is in Jerusalem near the Sheep Gate a pool, which in Aramaic is called Bethesda and which is surrounded by five covered colonnades. Here a great number of disabled people used to lie - the blind, the lame, the paralyzed. One who was there had been an invalid for thirty-eight years. When Jesus saw him lying there and learned that he had been in this condition for a long time, he asked him, "Do you want to get well?" John 5: 1-6 (NIV)

It is very important that we choose to recover. Not everyone makes that choice - you can spend the rest of your life mourning your loss. No one else can make this decision for you and no one else can do your "grief work." Unless you take responsibility for your own recovery, you will not recover. You must answer the questions: "Do you want to be well? Do you want to recover?" Books, counselors, groups, and friends can help you in the process. But only you can make the decision that you want to work through the grieving journey to healing.

How to start on the path toward recovery
1. Find a group or partner (someone who has experienced a similar loss)
    > It is imperative that you have support. It is very difficult to recover alone. Find a friend who understands, or a group which provides a safe, loving, nonjudgmental environment. The fact that you are in this group indicates that you have taken the first step.

2. Make a commitment to recover
    > Be committed to work through your grief journey
    > Be committed to stay with your grief group until you have recovered
    > Be honest about your feelings and take time to understand your emotions
    > Be willing to seek pastoral or professional help, if needed

3. Be willing to recognize non-productive behavior
    > Taking alcohol or medication to numb the pain
    > Considering the decision not to continue living (thoughts of suicide)
    > Overeating or not eating
    > Sleeping too much or too little

4. Recognize feelings of regret or guilt

    Almost immediately after the death of a loved one, grievers may start to think about things that they wish had been different, things they should have done or said, lost opportunities. Grieving people often experience the "If only's...": "If only I had insisted that he go to the doctor sooner," "If only we had taken that vacation that she wanted." "If only we had talked more." Memories of past hurts or pain, as well as perceived lost opportunities, are often the basis for deep feelings of regret or guilt.

5. Deal with your regrets

    How do we deal with these feelings of regret and guilt? Where there is real guilt over genuine misdeeds in the past, there is no shortcut but to acknowledge them and ask God's forgiveness. If you realize that you did the best that you could in the past, there is no need for regret. Sometimes pastoral counseling or sharing your feelings with another person makes it easier. As long as you hold on to your regrets you cannot move forward. You must be able to forgive yourself and others for the past.

Your decision: Will you make the decision to recover?

This is not easy - it means taking a realistic inventory of your feelings and taking the time to talk through them with another person, or sharing them with the group. It means taking time to understand yourself and your grief. It means making the commitment to continue the journey to recovery.

Questions:

1. What specific non-productive behavior have you experienced?

2. Do you have any regrets about a part of your relationship with your spouse?

3. Are you able to believe you did the best you could?

4. Have you been able to forgive yourself for the past?

5. Have you made the decision to recover?

Personal prayer at home:

If you have regrets, confess your feelings to God and ask His forgiveness. Let His comforting Spirit flow through you and feel His forgiveness and peace. Let go of your regret and any guilt you may feel.

THERE IS HOPE
YOU CAN RECOVER
YOU WILL SURVIVE AND LIVE AGAIN

*Rejoice in the Lord always. I will say it again: Rejoice! Let your gentleness
be evident to all. The Lord is near. Do not be anxious about anything, but in
everything, by prayer and petition, with thanksgiving, present your requests
to God. And the peace of God, which transcends all understanding, will guard
your hearts and your minds in Christ Jesus. Philippians 4: 4-7 (NIV)*

Week 6   Reconciling with the Past

Understanding our past losses

How we react to a serious loss often reflects how we have dealt with losses in our past. A helpful exercise is to think back to previous losses (family pets, your grandparents, other relatives) and remember how you reacted to them. It is likely that we continue to unconsciously react the same way each time we face loss. If you can remember how you dealt with past losses, it may help you to understand some of the ways you have been coping with this current loss.

Sometimes we discover that there are losses for which we have not completely grieved. Were you able to grieve sufficiently in the past or is there still pain over a past loss?

If you were not able to complete your grieving in the past, it may be because you were not able to satisfactorily conclude the relationship or say goodbye. Perhaps it was because of things unsaid or incomplete between you. This can be called an emotionally incomplete relationship. In order to resolve such an emotionally incomplete loss, you must be able to forgive, to say what is needed, and to let go. If you have not been able to complete your grieving for a loss in the past, you can still complete it now. You can do it alone. **If you are able to complete your emotional relationship, and let go of the past, it does not mean you'll have to forget your loved one.**

It is also possible that you had an incomplete relationship with your spouse at the time of death; that you were unable to say goodbye to him or her, or that there were some unresolved issues in your relationship.

When we aren't able to say goodbye; completing an incomplete farewell

If you had a good relationship with your spouse and there was time to talk before death occurred, you may have been able to say your goodbyes and now have a sense of completeness of the relationship. However, for many people, there may be some factors that can contribute to a feeling of emotional incompleteness:

Your spouse died suddenly, without time to express feelings

There were some unresolved problems in the marriage

There were things you wish you had said, or hadn't said

There were things you regret or would have done differently

How to identify an incomplete farewell

The first step is to find out what seems incomplete. What do we wish we had said or hadn't said? We often wish that things could have been different or better. Make a list of all the things you wish you had said but didn't. Make a list of things that you regret about the past. What would you have done differently?

How to forgive others and ourselves

At the heart of completing our relationships is forgiveness of the things we need to forgive ourselves or others for, whether real or imagined. Forgiving people does not mean endorsing their actions. But now is the time to forgive them and let go. It is important for you to recognize your part in not discussing issues or expressing feelings.

Recognize that you did the best you could at the time. The same is true for our loved ones. They did the best they could, too. It may not have been ideal, but it is your reality. Forgiveness is healing.

Dealing with anger

You may be angry with the person who died. It is important to resolve that anger. Some reasons for anger:

Feelings of abandonment ("Why did you leave me?")

Untimeliness of death ("You weren't supposed to die now")

Incomplete estate planning ("What am I going to do with the business?")

Panic ("How can I live without you?")

Expressing your feelings

An important part of recovery communication is expressing significant emotional statements. We may not have been able or had the time to say "I love you", "I am proud of you", "I don't want you to leave me", "I'm sorry about what happened", "I'm still angry with you". Whatever it was that we were unable to communicate in the past, we can communicate now. Make a list of all the things you want to say to your lost one. If you could have your loved one back for one last conversation, what would you want to say? What would you want to hear from your spouse?

When you know what you want to say, you need to communicate it. Some psychologists suggest talking to an empty chair, a beloved stuffed animal, or a close friend. One of the best ways to communicate is by writing a letter to your loved one. Using your list, write a letter, expressing what you need to say. You may feel pain, but it's okay to cry and to feel bad. Make sure you say everything that needs to be said. Be as complete as you can. Over time, you might want to write multiple letters.

Saying goodbye

When you have written your letter, read it out loud alone or with a friend. If you choose to be with a friend, tell your partner about the last conversation you had with your loved one. Pretend that he or she is really there. Read your letter out loud. Trust that this will work. If you start crying, keep going. If you're the listener, don't interrupt. When you get to the end of the letter and say "I love you", then it's time to tell your loved one goodbye. Not goodbye to the loving memories, but goodbye to the pain, confusion, and anguish. You'll feel an enormous sense of relief. You can now say farewell to your spouse and begin to move on.

Questions:

1. Make a list of all the past losses in your life and how you reacted to them. If you still have an emotional attachment to a loss, you may not have fully grieved that loss. Now is the time to complete that relationship and say goodbye to the relationship that is over without forgetting the role they played in your life.

2. Were you able to say goodbye to your loved one, or is your loss incomplete emotionally? Are there things you still need to say to your loved one?

3. Did you write your letter? If you did not write a letter or share it with someone, what do you think you could do to achieve a sense of completion of the relationship with your loved one? (See **Writing a Goodbye Letter** on page 43).

Personal prayer at home:

Ask God to let you release the pain and tell your loved one goodbye.

GRIEF RECOVERY

THERE IS HOPE
YOU CAN RECOVER
YOU WILL SURVIVE AND LIVE AGAIN

*As the Father has loved me, so have I loved you. Now remain in my love. If
you keep my commands, you will remain in my love, just as I have kept my
Father's commands and remain in his love. I have told you this so that my joy
may be in you and that your joy may be complete. John 15: 9-11 (NIV)*

Week 7   Turning the Corner

Now we can look back to see where we have been. We have passed through the first shock
of loss, begun to understand how little prepared we were to deal with our grief, and survived
the sadness of the second crisis when reality came crashing in. We have made the decision
to recover and have some knowledge of the journey through grief. We may have identified
incomplete relationships and prior incomplete grieving of past losses. We have learned how
to say farewell to our loved ones.

Now we can begin to be aware of how our lives have changed. Not just that our partner is
gone, but the other changes in our lives. We are learning to take care of ourselves. We are
more aware of loneliness, but we need this time to be alone and come to terms with all that
we have experienced. We have learned that although we will always miss our loved ones, he
or she will always be with us in our hearts and memories.

We can now be aware that we are ready to:

> Recognize our grieving as a positive and healing period in our lives
> Recognize avoidance behavior (being unduly busy, dependency on drugs)
> Recognize our anger and choosing to let go of it
> Resolve any remaining medical questions about the death
> Learn to be alone and start to appreciate the value of being alone
> Realize that it is healthy to begin to rely on yourself
> Be practical: there are things still to be handled

Looking from the past toward the future

From this point we can start to look toward the future. Before, there was no future.

> "My husband and I were both planners – short and long term. When he died
> suddenly and unexpectedly at 59, I felt like my future calendar was cut off.
> I kept thinking I could go back and change things. Then I was forced to live
> totally in the present. Surprisingly, that turned out to be an incredible gift
> during my journey of grief."

Now we are able to lift our heads and see that we will survive each day. Because we have made the choice to recover, we are willing to move into a new phase with new challenges.

This phase of the grieving journey includes:

> Recognizing that you have survived
> Being able to make an assessment of where you are
> Seeing your life as a continuing process
> Choosing to live, not to remain in the past
> Deciding not to be a victim
> Acknowledging that you are responsible for your own happiness
> Starting to rebuild your relationship with God, if it has faltered
> Taking responsibility for your future

What we need to do:

> Distinguish the difference between loneliness and solitude
> Remember the past without pain
> Acknowledge both the bad and the good in our relationship with the lost person
> Release resentment, anger, and guilt
> Shift our focus from what has happened to the future

How to help yourself:

> Let people around you know that you are committed to starting a second life and that you would appreciate their help and their support.

Your decision:

> To accept that you can say goodbye without forgetting the loved one
> To learn to manage your life alone
> To be willing to make the changes in your life that will enable you to grow

Questions:

1. Do a personal inventory:

Have you been able to let go of anger?

Are you still constantly sad?

Are you feeling extreme loneliness? What can you do about your loneliness?

Are you afraid of the future?

2. What positive decisions have you made about your life?

3. Is anything preventing you from moving forward?

4. What could you do to remove these obstacles?

5. Can you see a new life in the future?

6. Write down elements of what you want/feel your new life will be.

Personal prayer at home:
Ask God to help you move ahead toward wholeness.

GRIEF RECOVERY

THERE IS HOPE
YOU CAN RECOVER
YOU WILL SURVIVE AND LIVE AGAIN

"I am the vine; you are the branches. If you remain in me and I in you, you will bear much fruit; apart from me you can do nothing. John 15: 4-5 (NIV)

Week 8   Finding a New Place in Life

At this point you may feel confusion. Some of the extreme pain may have passed; you no longer live every moment of the day in despair. There is hope that you will recover from the pain of grief. But recover to what? Your old life is gone, never ever to return as before. The vast hole in your life that your spouse's death has caused is still there. How can you go on? What will life be like?

Your direction may be unclear, but one thing that is clear is that your role in life has shifted. For some, it may be a drastic change; for others, only minor. But there are definitely changes that you must adjust to.

During this time of finding a new direction you may experience:
> A growing realization that your life has changed in many ways
> A reluctance to make the necessary changes in your life
> Adjustment to the loss of your role as a spouse
> A realization that you are responsible for your own happiness
> A feeling of continuing loneliness
> A realization that you must look toward the future and let go of the past

What we can do at this time:
> Identify non-productive emotions: self-pity, anger, fear
>
> Recognize that loneliness is a choice:
>> We can be lonely because we do not choose to have friends
>> We can be lonely because we choose to remain in the past, waiting for
>>> our spouse (or spouse substitute) to return
>> Or we can reach out to others for friendship and companionship
>
> Find new roles:
>> Your former role as husband or wife no longer exists. There is not even the designation of "ex" that divorced people have. Your spouse is simply gone. You are a newly "single" person - an unfamiliar word when applied to you. You feel caught between two worlds and not fitting in either. You may wonder who you are.

27

Distinguishing between your roles and your identity.

What is a *role*? It is a social behavior pattern usually determined by our status in a particular society. It is relational. You have a role in your work, as a parent, as a spouse. Our roles may change by circumstances.

What is your *identity*? It is your individuality. It is what determines who you are, your character, your personality. It is what makes you different from every other human being. We receive our real identity from God - we are His children. He designed us. We can grow in our character, but essentially, we remain the same. Identity is what you are deep inside yourself, your innermost being.

Your decision: You must choose to understand yourself, take action, and plan what you are going to do.

Questions:

1. Has your perception of yourself changed since your loss?

2. How do others perceive you? Differently than before? Be specific.

3. Describe who you really are (your *identity*).

4. Describe/list your current **roles**. What additional roles have you assumed since your spouse died? What roles have you had to assign or completely drop?

5. Can you distinguish between your **identity** and your **roles**?

6. How can you be more yourself rather than trying to fit other people's idea of who you should be?

Personal prayer at home:

Ask God to help you discover your true identity as His child.

GRIEF RECOVERY

THERE IS HOPE
YOU CAN RECOVER
YOU WILL SURVIVE AND LIVE AGAIN

*"For I know the plans I have for you," declares the Lord, "plans to prosper you
and not to harm you, plans to give you a hope and a future. Then you will call
upon me and come and pray to me, and I will listen to you. You will seek me and
find me when you seek me with all your heart." Jeremiah 29: 11-13 (NIV)*

Week 9   Building a New Life

This is a time of reevaluating where we have been - looking at our past life, our loss, our
grieving. It is also a time when we must choose to look ahead to what can be for us. We do
have a choice: we can stay within the confines of our past, always in grief, always in pain, or
we can have the courage to find a new life. It will not be like the past. In some ways it will
never be as good; in some ways it will be better. It is not disloyal to your loved one to enjoy
your new life. It is not disloyal to choose to be happy. We will always carry our loved one with
us, as we carry memories of our parents, grandparents, and others who have died. But it is
important that we continue to complete our own lives. God has a plan for each of us, and we
must seek to find that plan to live by it. The tapestry of our lives has not yet been completed;
we must pick up the threads and continue to weave.

What we find as we look at the future:

New hopes and ambitions
That we are still dealing with fear of the future
Learning that we will have to take some risks
Not being afraid to fail at new ventures
Realizing that the old comforting support system is no longer there
Learning to manage our lives
Realizing that the grief will recur at intervals and that it is normal
Learning from the past and integrating it into our future life
Incorporating the memories of our loved one into our life
Letting go of our spouse without losing what he or she meant to us

Our focus as we integrate the past with the future

Connecting the threads of the past with the future
Internalizing the lost person

What do we mean by "internalizing the lost person"? When we have just lost
someone to death, there is a time when we feel very close physically to that
person. Active grieving maintains that closeness, and there are sometimes fears
that if we stop grieving, we will lose that last bond. But slowly, as we let go of
the grieving and begin to remember more objectively what we recall about that

31

person, we bring what we remember into our inner selves where we can carry our memories in our hearts without pain. It means being able to remember and talk about your lost spouse with a loving fondness. The past is not lost, but has become part of you and your life. It means bringing together the past and the present so there is no longer a division - no longer a time before death or a time after. All of this is your life, and your lost spouse will always be part of that life.

Areas of special difficulty:

The family unit – with some deaths, many family dynamics may totally change; a new family system must be devised, new roles accepted.

With the death of a husband or wife, the survivor becomes a single parent. This is difficult when there are small children or teenagers, but it also changes the dynamics of the family with adult children. During the earlier part of the grief journey, adult children may believe that taking over some responsibilities is helpful; however, this can create an unhealthy dependence. What is helpful is maintaining a delicate balance and remembering to return responsibilities when the grieving parent is ready.

Loss through failed marriage or divorce

Not every marriage is a happy one. There are situations where the couple has been separated or divorced, but the loss by death can still be traumatic. Issues of anger, unresolved conflicts, or uncompleted communications may need to be resolved. The grieving process can be just as difficult for the separated or divorced spouse as for the spouse in a successful marriage.

How to help yourself:

We need people around us who indicate that they know we have issues to work through to reestablish ourselves in life, but that they also know we are capable of meeting and resolving these issues.

Your decision:

You must choose to work through the conflicts between past and future.

Questions:

1. As you work through your problems, which are the most difficult for you? Place them in these categories:

        Practical Problems: Possible Solutions:

        Relational (People) Problems: Possible Solutions:

        Problems I can't do anything about:

2. Are you willing to look for new solutions to problems?

3. Can you accept the problems you can't do anything about?

4. As you have advanced in your grief journey, volunteering in your community can be a wonderful way to start new adventures and experiences while also meeting new people and beginning your new life.

The following tool has two parts: 1) A grid to look at characteristics that may indicate your personality style; and 2) Using the results of part 1, focus first on the quadrant that maps with the highest number of your characteristics. This might help you find a better fit for volunteering (or even a new career or new life purpose).

Fill out **A Quick Look at Your Personality Style** and **Check Any Volunteer Activities. . .** (See pages 45 & 47)

    In which quadrant do you primarily reside?

    ___ Practical Organizers   ___ Innovative Analyzers
    ___ Hands-On Makers   ___ Creative Helpers

    What volunteer opportunities have sparked an interest? A new career?

Personal prayer at home:
Share your fears of the future with God and ask Him for courage to take new risks in your life.

GRIEF RECOVERY

THERE IS HOPE
YOU CAN RECOVER
YOU WILL SURVIVE AND LIVE AGAIN

*Blessed be the God and Father of our Lord Jesus Christ, the Father of mercies
and God of all comfort; who comforts us in all our affliction so that we may
be able to comfort those who are in any affliction with the comfort with
which we ourselves are comforted by God. 2 Corinthians 1: 3 (NASB)*

Week 10   Getting Back in Balance

It is important to know that the grieving journey does not last for only 10 weeks. It will likely take two, three or even more years. But it is also important to know that recovery from the pain of grief is possible. It is possible to once again have fun, laugh, do exciting things, and be happy. Although it may seem highly unlikely at this point, it is even possible to meet someone else and begin a new life together. It is important to reach the point where the pain of grief has substantially diminished before embarking on a new relationship.

The grief journey toward recovery takes time – more than you want it to and more than our current culture accepts. It cannot be rushed through. The more thoughtfully you proceed, the better the results will be. Your task now is to begin to integrate your grief experiences into your whole life and look to the future.

There are some positive feelings:

Joy, satisfaction, and a sense of accomplishment
Return to a steady state of balance
Increased capacity to appreciate people and things
More tolerance and understanding of others' grief
Desire to find new friendships and relationships
A sense of play and freedom
A deepening of your faith

Some new life experiences:

Finding deeper resources of strength
Learning self-management
Choosing to fully participate in life
Discovering that living in the present can be joyful
Knowing that life will always be full of change
Being able to evaluate change
Finding contentment through God's love
Accepting your own mortality
Seeking a new purpose for your life

Establishing new relationships

Having a more positive view of life - Choosing to be happy

Moving beyond loss

When your spouse died, his or her life came to an end. You are a survivor - you have a life to complete. In the tapestry of your life, one strand ended, another continues. Life as you knew it may not exist anymore, and you have been given the chance for a new life.

What you make of it is up to you. If this sounds like another choice, it is. You can choose to remain static, not moving forward, or you can move on with your life.

What you do with the rest of your life depends upon how actively you seek new goals and new purpose for your life. It takes a lot of time to recover from traumatic grief. Don't be impatient. Take your time. When the time comes to "pick up your mat and walk", you will know that you are ready. Don't be surprised if the sadness revisits you from time to time - chances are, it always will. But knowing that your grieving has been necessary and cleansing, you can be confident that a new life awaits you.

In conclusion:

In these 10 weeks we have accomplished much. We have:

Acknowledged that we are in pain

Faced our loss

Understood why the world views us as it does

Recognized that the grief returns again and again

Remembered our past losses

Looked for the first time at the future

Decided to let change happen in our lives

We are beginning to:

Understand our own grieving journey

Let go of our loved ones who have died

Say goodbye in the midst of our remembering

Discover new roles

Integrate our past with our future

Feel back in balance

Move beyond loss

Recovering from the death of a loved one is one of the most difficult things we will ever have to face, and is physically, emotionally, and spiritually exhausting. We have had every reason to feel lost. But with the help of God and the support of others who understand our pain we do have hope and know that we will recover from the pain of grief. Together we can continue to walk through the grieving journey and will not only survive, but fully live again.

Questions:

1. Where do you think you are now in your grieving process? (Place a mark on the line)

Date of Death   A New Future

_____

2. Are you able to see a new horizon? If so, what do you see?

3. Do you believe you can now begin to draw on what you have learned to comfort others and to help others to understand their loss?

Personal prayer at home:

Thank God for His support in guiding you through this part of your grieving process. Ask for His continued guidance.

GRIEF RECOVERY

A Christian Perspective of the Grieving Process

Losing a spouse to death is an event of tragic proportions. Whether the death came suddenly or after a lengthy illness, we are never prepared. Whether the marriage had been strong or troubled, the loss is equally devastating. Our individual marriages were as different as we are from one another, yet the pain of bereavement is equally deep. We may have different circumstances surrounding our lives and the death of our spouse, yet we share much in common. Grief is irrespective of social differences - we all hurt.

So, what is grieving? Does all this pain serve any purpose? Is there a pattern to my grieving? Will the pain ever go away? And the biggest question of all: Why did this happen?

The believing Christian often has a difficult time with this question of "Why?" We believe in a loving God through whom *"all things work together for the good of those who love him, who have been called according to his purpose." (Romans 8: 28 NKJV).* How can it be good that He has taken our loved one away? How do you reconcile your faith with the loss of your loved one? How can you work through this pain to reach a place of acceptance where your life can continue and you can trust God again?

We believe that God has given us the grieving process for the purpose of enabling us to understand and accept our loss. The Lord was no stranger to grief. Of the coming Messiah, Isaiah says, *"He was despised and rejected by mankind, a man of sorrows, and familiar with grief." (Isaiah 53:3 NIV).* Jesus wept at the tomb of Lazarus, and he wept over Jerusalem. He understands our confusion and grief.

We also believe that grieving is a God-given healing process that will lead you from darkness into light, if you choose to make it happen and ask God to help you. There are some who reject grieving and settle into a state of denial of their grief. They may live for years in this denial, but at the cost of their own emotional freedom and spiritual growth. The choice is up to you whether you will flee from your grief or walk through the grieving process to recovery.

Frequently we feel that God is not with us, in our grief we cry out, "Where are you, Lord?" Yet as time passes, we can look back and see that the Lord was indeed with us, carrying us through our spiritual and emotional darkness. It is we who can't see God and who are blinded by our pain, for His Word says, *"I will never leave you nor forsake you." (Joshua 1:5 NIV).*

A helpful analogy of the grieving process occurs in *Psalm 23:4-6 (NKJ) "Yea, though I walk through the valley of the shadow of death, I will fear no evil, for You are with me; Your rod and Your staff, they comfort me."* Choosing to walk through grief is walking through this dark valley. But when we climb up out of the valley, we can be in the light of hope once again. God will walk with us through our pain, if we will let Him minister to us through prayer and the ministry of others.

GRIEF RECOVERY

COMMON GRIEF REACTIONS

This table lists symptoms commonly expected during bereavement. Each person will experience a unique blend of some or all of these symptoms listed and perhaps some that are not listed.

PHYSICAL	EMOTIONAL	MENTAL
Pain Fatigue, exhaustion, low energy Sleep and appetite disruption Shortness of breath Tight or heavy feeling in chest Feeling of tightness in throat Hollow feeling in stomach Stomach pain and upset Heartache, broken heart Dry mouth Tension Restlessness, irritability Increased sensitivity to stimuli "Grief Attacks" "Sympathy pains" Accident prone	Shock, numbness, emptiness Sadness Sorrow for the one who died Loneliness, longing, yearning Anger, resentment Guilt, shame, regret, remorse "More I should have done" Fear, anxiety, insecurity Feeling helpless, out of control Diminished self-concern "Don't care," "What does it matter" Depression Desire to join the deceased Suicidal feelings Feelings of betrayal, disloyalty "Emotional roller coaster" Relief	Disbelief Confusion Disorientation Absentmindedness Forgetfulness Poor concentration Easily distracted Difficulty focusing and attending Low motivation Expecting to see the deceased Expecting the deceased to call Preoccupation with the deceased Need to tell and retell story Dreams or images of the deceased Denial Thinking about other deaths and losses
SOCIAL	**BEHAVIORS**	**SPIRITUAL**

Being isolated from others
Withdrawing from social activities
Diminished desire for conversation
Being "widowed," "single," etc.
Hide grief to "take care of others"
Family relationships strained
Lose friends, make new friends
Redefining oneself
	Crying (sometimes unexpectedly)
	Searching
	Carrying special objects
	Going to grave site
	Making and keeping an altar
	Keeping belongings intact
	Looking at photos or videos
	Listening to tapes
	Talking to the deceased
	Avoiding situations that arouse
	   grief
	Changes in daily routine
	"Staying busy"
	Assuming mannerisms of the
	   deceased
		Questions about God:
		   Why would God allow this?
		Angry at God
		Questions about the deceased:
		   Where are they now?
		   Are they OK?
		   Can they see me?
		   Will I see them again?
		   What will happen when I die?
		Sensing the deceased's presence
		Hearing, smelling, or seeing the
		   deceased
		Death affirms or challenges
		   beliefs
		Awe, wonder, mystery
		Continuing relationship with the
		   deceased

©1997 Compiled by Howard Lunche, LCSW
©2021 With permission, updated by Merrilee Harter Mitchell
P. O. Box 5811 Berkeley, CA 94705
510-841-2930

GRIEF RECOVERY

Writing a Goodbye Letter

Dear. . .

- Wonderful memories of you and our life together that I cherish

- Thoughts and feelings I experienced at the time of your death

- Things I miss about you

- Things I wish I could have said and done before you died

- Thoughts about hurts, problems, and/or disappointments we experienced in our life together

- Things about your death that I think were partly my fault

- Things I regret about our relationship

- Things for which I am angry at you

- Things I need to ask forgiveness for or to forgive

- How your death has affected my life

- Important events that have occurred since you died that I wish you could have experienced, or that I would like to have shared with you

- How I feel about you today

- How I feel about my life now – good and not so good

- Other thoughts and feelings I want to include in this letter to you

(This is a partial list, pick those that are appropriate for you now. You might want to write more in future letters.)

GRIEF RECOVERY

A Quick Look at Your Personality Style

1) Check Characteristics that Reflect Your Natural, Comfortable Style

2) Check as many or as few (including "0") characteristics in each section

#1 I.	#3 I. . . . .
__ Value stability, duty, service, structure	__ Like to design complex systems
__ Am responsible, loyal, decisive: work hard	__ Analyze, give critical feedback
__ Am prepared, organized, dependable	__ Like to solve theoretical problems
__ Meet deadlines, follow-through	__ Use intuitive creativity & logic to innovate
__ Trust facts, logic, proven results	__ Value expertise and independence
__ Am precise, detail-oriented	__ Like to debate/argue different points of view
__ Value saving time/money, efficiency	__ Like to make systems more efficient
__ Value measurable results	__ Like to brainstorm new ideas, future trends
__ Value logic and am also people-sensitive	__ Am calm, reasonable, logical, concise
__ Value being objective	__ Am objective, direct, efficient
#2 I.	**#4 I. . . . .**
__ Am spontaneous, flexible, practical	__ Am friendly, personal, positive
__ Learn-by-doing; learn hands-on	__ Enjoy interacting with people
__ Want to see tangible results	__ Like to help people grow & develop
__ Am good with my hands, good at crafts	__ Am insightful about people
__ Take action now to solve problems quickly	__ Like to give, receive appreciation for caring
__ Like excitement, fun, urgency, risk-taking	__ Am creative about helping people
__ Want direct, specific, relevant information	__ Want to contribute, make a difference
__ Make clever solutions based on past results	__ Value harmony, community, creativity
__ Am good at troubleshooting & crises	__ Like to collaborate, be on teams
__ Value action and am people-sensitive	__ Support agreement; avoid criticism
	__ Adapt my style to different situations

What Does this Quiz Reflect About Me?

1) **The section where you made the most checks may be your main personality style**

2) **Other sections with a number of checks may reflect another important part of your personality or a style you adapt and use for work or social situations**

Adapted by Linda Artel

GRIEF RECOVERY

Check Any Volunteer Activities that Appeal To You
They May Relate to Your Main Personality Style or to Another Part of You that You Want to Explore by Volunteering. Check whatever works for you and add more!

#1 Practical Organizers
__ Help low-income people with taxes
__ Be treasurer or secretary for a non-profit
__ Serve on a budget committee
__ Organize fundraising events
__ Be a substance abuse counselor
__ Be a hospice volunteer
__ Provide credit counseling
__ Serve on the board of a non-profit
__ Provide services for the elderly
__ Teach students about personal finance
__ Advise small businesses (i.e. with SCORE*)
__ Run for local political office or school board
__ Help w/administrative matters at your place of worship
__ Help international aid organization with logistics
__ Work with organization that helps lost pets
__ Volunteer in a healthcare setting
__ Help in a special education class
__ Teach as a religious educator
__ Add your own:

#3 Innovative Analyzers
__ Write, edit a non-profit website or podcast
__ Design or code a website
__ Serve as board member, planning strategy & policy
__ Develop and implement new programs or special projects
__ Write proposals to seek funding for an organization
__ Volunteer as social entrepreneur with a non-profit start-up
__ Do Information Technology work for a non-profit
__ Tutor students in science, math or other subjects you like
__ Lead tours as a science docent
__ Use professional skill i.e. legal, technical, for a non-profit
__ Advise a start-up business (i.e. with SCORE*)
__ Do research, strategy or PR for a political campaign
__ Write and/or give speeches for an issue or campaign
__ Develop or enhance fundraising plan for a non-profit
__ Direct a community theater production
__ Use your skills to help an international aid organization
__ Voice critical opinions on social media
__ Add your own:

#2 Hands-On Makers
__ Deliver food or cook for the elderly or disabled
__ Join volunteer fire fighting unit
__ Work with the Sea Scouts
__ Lead young people on wilderness trips
__ Build/repair homes with organizations like Habitat
__ Repair used computers for low-income students
__ Work at a crisis center or on a hot-line
__ Train/work as volunteer emergency support
__ Coach a youth team in your favorite sport
__ Volunteer at a national/state/regional park
__ Install computer networks for schools
__ Set-up sound equipment for fundraisers
__ Work backstage for drama group
__ Tutor or be teacher's assist. for technical/math subjects
__ Help create/maintain a community or school garden
__ Organize, Promote or host a fundraising event
__ Help international group create/sell crafts
__ Help with hospice care
__ Train dogs to aid people with disabilities
__ Help young people do craft projects
__ Train to run/cycle/swim for fundraising events
__ Be a Big Sister or Big Brother
__ Add your own:

#4 Creative Helpers
__ Be an art museum docent
__ Volunteer at a library
__ Recruit/motivate volunteers in person & with social media
__ Use artistic skills to help a non-profit
__ Join community drama or dance group
__ Collaborate w/team to organize a fundraising event
__ Create a non-profit that fills an unmet community need
__ Be a mentor, Big Sister or Big Brother
__ Tutor or be a teacher's assistant; teach literacy
__ Promote fundraising events through social media
__ Recruit new members for a non-profit
__ Work for candidate or cause you support
__ Direct or be part of a music group, choir, band
__ Help with bilingual education
__ Volunteer at a pre-school or after school program
__ Help an organization working with troubled adolescents
__ Do teambuilding or diversity workshops for a non-profit
__ Create/Plan conference on an important issue-work w/a team
__ Volunteer to help (and participate) at a spiritual retreat
__ Research/write/video/blog about an issue important to you
__ Be a court-appointed foster child advocate (CASA**)
__ Use creative people skills to help international organization
__ Add your own:

*SCORE = Service Corps of Retired Executives
**CASA = Court Appointed Special Advocate

Adapted by Linda Artel

GRIEF RECOVERY

How to Survive the Holidays

There are really only two ways to deal with special days and holidays: flee them or face them. There is nothing wrong with leaving town and doing something entirely different. It is equally OK to stay and see it through, even though there may be some pain involved. However, it is hard to escape the prologue to the holidays. Easter seems to start in January, the Fourth of July looms large all summer, plans for Thanksgiving get under way in September, and Christmas, Hanukah, and Kwanza start in October! So, the pressure mounts. We have to make decisions about where we will be, what we will do, who we will see. This can be very painful as we seek to reconcile the past with the present. It is important that we learn to deal with holidays, as they are a yearly occurrence, and each year we must face them anew.

There are choices you can make to help you through the tough times. It is not necessary to be miserable - in fact you may find new ways to enjoy the holiday time.

Here are some suggestions for you as the holidays approach:

1. Recognize that the holidays may be difficult for you as memories come sweeping back. Don't let them creep up on you. Be prepared.

2. Realize that there will be some pain and sadness and that there are no magical solutions. Plan your days ahead of time so that you aren't too stressed or too lonely.

3. Don't try to do too much. You don't have to prove anything to yourself or anyone. Give yourself time to rest and be with people you love.

4. Don't be afraid to make changes. Now is the time to let go of old traditions and start some new ones. On the other hand, if doing things the same way is more comfortable, do it.

5. Let your family and friends know about your feelings. Don't just go along with their plans. Get together early in the season to decide what you are going to do and then stick with it.

6. Let others take more of the responsibility for gatherings and food. You don't have to provide everything for everybody. Don't feel guilty - learn to say "No."

7. Do your shopping early. If you don't feel like exchanging gifts, you may want to eliminate it this year. Be flexible.

8. Don't neglect your health. Eat sensibly and get regular exercise.

9. Be sure you have some plans for Hanukah, Christmas Eve or New Year's Eve. Don't be alone. Invite some friends for dinner. Attending a church service with friends may help start your new year with hope.

10. Center your activities and thoughts more on the real meaning of Christmas. Let God comfort you during His own special time of year.

What to do about:

Christmas Cards

    If you decide to send cards, start writing them early.

    You can choose not to send cards this year; your friends will understand.

    Writing a letter instead of sending cards might feel more appropriate.

Christmas Music

    Be prepared to hear carols when you are shopping or in public places.

    Use your own music in the car and at home.

    Choose some new music to listen to and enjoy.

Shopping and Gift Giving

    If you decide to give gifts, shop early to avoid stress.

    Remember that you have the option to not give gifts this year.

    Give only those gifts that you want to give: give from the heart.

    Don't give in to the pressure that you have to do more than you are able to do.

Holiday Decorating and Tree Trimming

    Do only what you feel like doing. This is not Homes and Gardens time.

    You may want to have the same size tree and decorate as usual. That's OK.

    If you have a tree, invite friends to help you decorate.

    Remember you have the option not to have a tree or to do something different.

    If you will be away during the holidays, don't bother with decorating.

Cooking

    If baking and cooking gives you pleasure, do it!

    If spending time in the kitchen is painful, forget it!

In all these matters, remember that you have the option to:

    1. Keep the old traditions

    2. Change the traditions

    3. Not to do anything

Remember, it's your decision!

GRIEF RECOVERY

Frequently Asked Questions

1. When should I take off my wedding rings?
There is no specific time period of mourning in our society, so it is up to you. Some people continue to wear their rings indefinitely; others wear them until a time when it seems appropriate to remove them. If removing them makes you feel uncomfortable, don't do it. You'll know when you're ready.

2. Is it appropriate to keep photos of the deceased spouse on view?
Why not? Your spouse was a central part of your life and you want to remember him or her. If it gives you pleasure to have photos around the house, then do so. Don't feel that you have to explain to visitors; it's not a symptom of abnormality. If relatives feel uncomfortable about photos, remind them that it is your house and you are able to make your own decisions.

3. How often should I go to the cemetery to visit the burial site?
Whenever it seems natural for you to do so. As time passes, you may find that the number of visits lessens. There are no rules about this and you don't need to explain to anyone.

4. When should I remove my spouse's clothing and personal belongings from the house?
Again, there is no set time limit on this. Some people feel better giving the clothing away soon after death; others wait a year or more. If you wait a long period of time, it does not necessarily mean that you are not recovering, only that you are not yet ready to undertake the task. Sometimes asking a friend or relative to help you may make it easier. As we get older, we have more losses, possibly an estate to settle and more personal effects to distribute. It should get easier, but often it's not.

5. What should I keep of my spouse's personal effects?
Whatever you want. Keep those things which are meaningful to you.

6. What about the furniture?
If you don't like the furniture that your spouse purchased, now is the time to replace it. You aren't being disloyal; you are rebuilding your life more in your image. If you like the decor just the way it is, by all means, don't change it. If you want something different, do it.

7. It's been almost a year, why am I feeling so weird?
We have learned that often, but not always, starting about six to eight weeks before the anniversary date of the death, widows and widowers experience increased emotional reactions that seem to be unexplainable. The body appears to have emotional memory and it is signaling the bereaved that the anniversary is coming. Usually, the actual anniversary day is not as hard as the weeks leading up to it. This is normal.

8. What about the anniversary of the death?

Most people mark the date by visiting the burial site either with friends and relatives or go alone. It might be significant to go with your children, if that is appropriate. You should prepare for the date and plan to be with someone who understands. It's OK to be sad and relive the events of the death and funeral. Part of the grieving journey is letting yourself feel your grief. Don't be surprised if you are somewhat depressed at this time of year. This will get better with time.

9. Why is the second year so hard?

While it is not always the case, many of our widows and widowers have reported that the second year is even more difficult than the first year. But it is difficult in very different ways. During the first year, much of the beginning months are spent in shock or a form of numbness. Also, as we are facing many events for the first time – birthdays, anniversaries, weddings, memorial services, holidays, etc. – we either isolate ourselves to avoid the pain, or we steel ourselves to have the fortitude to attend the events. Either way, as our journey continues into the second year, we begin to recognize that "this is the beginning of my new life and I don't like it." This is normal and is a healthy part of the journey through grief. It will get better as we travel further in our journey.

10. What about dating and marrying again?

See Week 10. If you have recovered from the pain of grief and feel like a whole person again and find someone who also is a whole person whom you can love and live with, it's a wonderful idea. It is not disloyal to your departed spouse. A new marriage can bring great joy to your life.

Caution: It is likely that as you finish this course, you are not whole yet. New widows and widowers can be very vulnerable. It is recommended that you not get seriously involved until you are whole. One-half of you and one-half of another do not make a whole person.

While you are single, spend your social time going out to meet new friends, not to meet a future mate. Go with groups who share a common interest – hiking, photography, dancing, theater, boating etc. Remember, unfortunately there are sharks out there and we are still vulnerable until we complete our grief journey. At that point, a new relationship can be wonderful.

GRIEF RECOVERY

How to Start and Lead a Widows and Widowers Ministry at Your Church

Introduction

The need for grief recovery groups in the church

Widows and widowers may sometimes be an overlooked segment of our churches. Dealing with grief and loss is difficult and the church staff may not be prepared to minister to the bereaved on a continuing basis. A Grief Recovery Support Group can help widows and widowers better understand their grieving process and enable them to not only recover from their pain of grief but guide them to a new purposeful and productive life.

Why widowed people are different from divorced people

Most single people are divorced. There are many more issues to consider if a person is divorced; there can be much bitterness or anger. Sometimes one party in a divorce did not want to end the marriage and therefore suffers the pain of rejection or desertion. Most have suffered financially and may be involved in long court disputes over child custody and/or support issues. Some parents have lost custody of their children. The ex-spouse must be dealt with, sometimes on a daily basis. These problems of the divorced are different from those of the bereaved and should be addressed in another program.

On the other hand, a person who has been widowed is coping with the pain of the involuntary loss of a loved one, sometimes after a long illness. The widow or widower's primary need is for comfort and hope that life can continue without the spouse. The immediate pain is numbing and life-shattering. Sometimes the bereaved are barely able to cope with the necessities of life, much less with the demands of working or settling an estate. Even after many months, many are unable to function really well. Those who return to work or seemingly have recovered, may actually still be suffering and need help.

Unfortunately, our society gives support to widows and widowers for only a short period of time after bereavement. Friends and relatives can be anxious for the survivor to get back to normal, and may have unrealistic expectations of the length of the grief journey.

What is recovery?

Recovery is defined as "to bring back to normal position or condition." For the bereaved, the concept of returning to "normal" may seem impossible. Therefore, recovery for the grieving can be interpreted as being able to continue living without experiencing the symptoms of extreme grief: continuous crying, sleeplessness, disorientation, depression, numbness, anger, being fearful of the future. Certainly, the sadness of the loss will remain, but the paralyzing blackness of despair is gone. A new marriage does not guarantee recovery; successful remarriage may follow recovery, but seldom or never precedes it. Recovery also evidences itself in renewed social interaction and renewed interest in living. Those who have recovered from the pain of grief can find a new "normalcy," are able to enjoy life once again, and can envision a new future.

Purpose of the support group

Giving hope for recovery

The first thing that the bereaved need is to be given hope. They need to be able to tell the story of their loss to sympathetic and empathetic listeners. They also need to repeat their story many times but often feel that they are burdening others with their grief. The tendency of widows and widowers is to retreat into their grief, feeling little desire to reach out to the world. If they remain alone with their grief, they may be vulnerable to emotional and physical decline. Those who must return to work may find that they can't concentrate. Many are subject to sudden bursts of crying and deep sadness.

By being in a support group, widows and widowers are able to express their feelings in a safe and nonjudgmental environment. They can cry and express anger. They hear others' stories and realize that they are not alone; others have had similar experiences and are surviving. As the weeks go by, the group members seem to find equilibrium and eventually are able to smile and even laugh about some of their experiences in dealing with widowhood.

Making a decision to recover

The most important factor in recovery is the widow or widower's decision to recover. It may be surprising, but there are those who chose not to recover. Many times, these are elderly Christian men or women who expected to precede their spouses in death and are now waiting to join their loved ones in heaven. They may have years of productive service ahead of them, but without encouragement, they seem to give up.

Younger people may find strength in toughing it out and denying their grief. They may try to fill their lives with activity, become overly busy and not take the time to understand their feelings. Frequently someone like this will come to a recovery class several years after their loss when they realize that they never completed their grieving.

Sometimes men may choose not to take the time to complete the grieving journey and instead set forth on a search for a wife replacement. The marriages that may result from the search are seldom successful. Often the new wife is much younger and has higher expectations of the marriage than the husband can provide, or the husband is surprised that the new wife doesn't meet his expectations. It is important that both men and women recover from their grieving and become whole people again before they embark upon new relationships. Certainly, it is impossible for anyone to completely replace the former spouse, although a new marriage can eventually bring much joy.

Part of the study in the group is examining this decision to recover. It requires a commitment; the first evidence is that of continuing to attend the group. Those who decide otherwise usually drop out after a week or two.

Emphasis on God's plan for our lives

"For I know the plans I have for you," declares the Lord, "plans to prosper you and not to harm you, plans to give you a hope and a future." Jeremiah 29:11 (NIV)

A continuous thread throughout the class should be the reference to God's plan for our lives. It is the best answer to "Why did God let my spouse die?" That was God's plan for his or her life. He has another plan for the survivor. This is extremely difficult for the widow or widower to grasp. In their view, they have lost fully half of themselves - almost as though a knife has severed them. The idea that this could be God's plan seems cruel. We can never explain God's ways, but we can learn to accept them without bitterness and anger. It is important that the bereaved see past the immediate pain, begin to trust God, and start to see ahead the hope of a new life.

Choosing a leader

The leader as a model of recovery

When choosing the person who will lead the group, it is important that credibility be a chief factor. Those in the group will trust and be most at ease with someone who has been through the same grieving experience. The leader must also be willing to openly share his or her grief experience with the group in order to win the trust of the group. By sharing parts of that experience, others will be encouraged to talk more freely about their grief.

The leader must be significantly recovered and emotionally mature

If the group members are to believe that they can recover, they must have a leader who is well on the path to recovering from the pain of grief. The leader must present a model of transformation in order that others may have hope. It is possible for someone who is still on the journey of recovery to lead the group, but he or she must have a thorough understanding of the grieving journey and know where they are. Someone who has been through a grief recovery workshop and is emotionally mature may be able to continue their recovery while leading the group, but the group must be aware of exactly where the leader is in his or her recovery. The leader must display complete openness, vulnerability, and honesty if he or she is to be trusted.

The leader must feel called by God and have a heart for the bereaved

Not everyone has a heart for the bereaved. It is a difficult ministry and requires empathy and compassion - although a certain tough-mindedness is helpful. The leader cannot be drawn into a dependent relationship with any of the group members, but must be able to lead the group without involvement. Those who have been most successful in leading church bereavement support groups have felt God's call to this ministry. The many challenges given by the group can be met through prayer and the help of the Holy Spirit.

The leader must be able to facilitate the group

The leader does not need to be a teacher, but should have basic skills in leading small groups and facilitating discussion. One of the challenges for the facilitator is keeping the group in balance; giving everyone an opportunity to express his or her feelings and ideas without monopolizing the sharing time. The leader should be able to encourage those who are quieter as well as being able to gently limit the more talkative members.

It is well to remember that this is not a therapy group, and anyone who seems to have deeper psychological problems should be referred to a professional for help.

How to organize and lead the group

Size and limitations of the group

Although it is possible to have as many as 20 group members, the ideal group number is 9 to 10 as it is easier to create an atmosphere of closeness with a smaller group. However, it's best not to limit the group initially, as there may be some attrition throughout the series; some people may decide that the group is not meeting their needs while others have other obligations or just drop out. It is very important that the group be urged to make a commitment to stay for the entire series, as this will facilitate their recovery.

Membership should be limited to only those who have lost spouses since the issues that widows and widowers face are unique and rapport in the group is best accomplished when all have shared the same experience. There may be others who have lost parents, children, siblings, fiancés, or even pets, who ask to join the group. Although the process of grieving is universal, the focus of this group is very specific and those who have other losses would be benefit more through a more general grief support group.

It is always a question whether or not to keep the group open to new members or whether to close the group after the second meeting (recommended). A newcomer after the second week can become an intrusion into a bonded group. On the other hand, an open group of attendees who knew each other before can also be effective as the "older" members comfort and reassure the newcomers. The principal problem with an open group is that the newcomer has not had the benefit of the prior weeks' study and sharing. It can be very difficult to catch up emotionally with the rest of the group.

Meeting times

A weekly series is best - it is hard to get the attention of deeply bereaved people and if the meetings are bimonthly or monthly, you will lose most of the members. They seem to be able to remember "every Tuesday night", but not "every other Tuesday night". It is important to have structure: start the meetings on time and end on time. A two to two and a half-hour meeting with a 15-minute coffee break seems to work well.

Meeting agenda

1. Sharing your story

The most important work that is done in a Grief Recovery Group is that of sharing. Generally, the first hour is spent with each person briefly telling his or her story, which is the narrative of the illness, death, and subsequent days following the death of their spouse. During the first meetings, more time is allowed for each story. Each week, the leader can ask for a briefer account, and then after 3 or 4 weeks, the sharing is more concerned with issues that have arisen during their grief journey.

2. Fellowship

Much of the healing seems to take place in the sharing and bonding of the group. Therefore, the coffee break should be as long as possible without taking time from the formal sharing and introduction of the material. During this time, group members have an opportunity to talk on a more intimate level and begin to form friendships which will carry over into their personal life. After 4 to 6 weeks, the fellowship aspect of the group becomes more important and they may be eager to start meeting socially outside of the group. The leader might suggest that they meet for coffee or dinner before or after the meeting - not always as a group (although that is an option), but with those with whom they have an affinity. If this is suggested, be aware of and discourage the formation of cliques as they can isolate others.

3. Learning about the grieving journey

The purpose of the workbook is twofold: to give some structure to the group meetings, and to instruct the members about their grieving journey. Once they see that there is a potential roadmap and a beginning and an end to grieving, they begin to believe that they can look forward to a meaningful life again. Since most of the bereaved have little hope that they will ever be able to regain what they consider normalcy, they must be given this hope that they can recover from the pain.

4. Preparation for a new personal life

The latter chapters of the workbook focus more on the changes that the group members will be facing in their lives. By the 8th week, they usually start asking questions about social life and are interested in moving forward with their lives. Those who have not progressed that far should be encouraged to repeat the series.

5. Prayer support

The one factor that a grief support group in a church can provide that secular groups cannot is the power of prayer. Although the group members may not all be believers (a group can come from a wide geographic area and not exclusively from the church), I recommend consistently ending the group time with a circle of prayer or a gratitude circle. Asking for prayer requests may be too time consuming, so the leader may ask each member to offer a sentence prayer of thanks or a request to God. Those who are non-believers or uncomfortable may be given the option to remain silent by just saying "pass." Many members may have no experience in praying aloud with others, but as time passes, they will be encouraged and perhaps begin to offer a short prayer. The leader can begin the prayer time by thanking the Lord for His goodness and faithfulness. A sense of bonding and closeness to God, even for the nonbelievers, can result from this fairly simple prayer time.

We end with hugs all around, even with those who are not used to Christian hugs. By the end of 10 weeks, almost all will be hug addicts. Besides the expression of friendship and compassion, many of the group may have had no physical contact with anyone since their spouse died. To be held in loving arms and comforted can be a moving experience for them and reinforces the idea of Christian fellowship.

Note: If the group is an all-Christian group, giving more time to individual prayer might be helpful. This group might then want to continue after the series as a fellowship or covenant group for continued support.

Workbook

Purpose of the workbook

When I first began the support group, I had planned to use a study of the Book of Job. I quickly discovered that the level of pain of the participants was so great that they couldn't concentrate on a Bible study and Job is not a helpful book to study during significant grief. It seemed evident that they needed material that would relate directly to their experiences. I had also initially considered leading an open, drop-in type of group. However, as time has passed, I have become even more convinced that a 10-week series, using a workbook, gives the group structure and a progressive movement toward recovery from the pain of grief.

Certainly no one will recover completely in 10 weeks, but it teaches him or her about recovery and prepares them for their continuing journey. Learning about their grieving journey, being able to share their stories, beginning to let go of the past, and starting to build a new life will encourage group members to believe that there will be eventual healing.

Books on grief

There are many excellent books about grieving, most of them recalling a personal experience of grief and a testimony about recovery. These are very helpful and are recommended for outside reading. Everyone seems to have a favorite book which has spoken to his or her heart and such reading should be encouraged. There are also resources which deal with the practical, financial, and legal matters which can accompany bereavement.

Initiating the program

Church bulletins, announcements, and brochures
The first step in letting people know about your group is placing an announcement in the church bulletin. If the church wants to extend the breadth of the group, an announcement in the local paper or information sent to other churches may bring good results. It is helpful to produce a brochure which can be distributed throughout church groups and can be mailed to interested parties. If producing a brochure is too difficult, a flyer or an attractively designed sheet of paper will do as well.

Many of the group members were initially contacted by friends or relatives who had seen an announcement or flyer about the group. Most group members come to the group through referrals from someone else; often someone who is in the deep sadness of grief will not respond to an announcement, therefore it is important that all members of the church be informed about the group. Also, an announcement from the pulpit may be an encouraging factor.

Contacting other churches, hospice and social workers
Besides mailing a brochure or flyer to local churches, another way to let other churches know about the group is by personal contact with someone who is in a visitation ministry, either a pastor or volunteer. A pastoral care pastor would be in a position to know about those who have been bereaved.

If you wish to extend the group membership as a form of outreach outside your church, another source of referrals can be social workers, especially those in hospice programs at local hospitals. I have also had referrals from professional counselors for their Christian clients. Many secular counselors recognize the value of support groups and faith in the recovery process.

Also ask church members to tell everyone they know about the group. It is amazing how news travels. Men and women have learned about the group by the most unusual means: from a neighbor who heard about the group from a friend, from a baby sitter who was in a youth group at the church, from a nurse in the hospital who heard about the group from a patient. Eventually, your community will become aware of the group.

Practical experiences

Recovery as a choice: recovery vs. non-recovery

It must be stressed throughout the series that recovery involves individual choice. Many people fear that if they recover, they will lose the last contact they have with their spouse; their grieving serves as a last bond. It is not true that if they recover, they will lose their memories - they will only lose the pain. This may be hard to understand and needs to be explained repeatedly.

It is also important to stress the potential for productivity and usefulness in life, not to mention the joy that the Lord gives us, when the choice is recovery. Those who are bereaved must be given a reason for living on without their loved one.

The intake process and attending the first few meetings

It is important for the facilitator to talk with each potential widow or widower attendee prior to the start of the group. Generally, they should be six months to two years into the journey of grief; however, the course has been successful for people who are much farther along. Often, if people who are 5-20 years into the process and are still grieving deeply, it is because they have not made the choice to recover from the pain of grief. During the intake conversation, it is helpful to have them tell their story and then to warn them that when they attend the first few meetings, they may feel worse when they leave than when they arrived. This is because we are opening the wounds that need complete healing and it is healthy and normal for that to happen. Be sure to suggest they commit to attend the first four meetings before making a decision to discontinue. Almost no one has left the group after three weeks and they all are glad they stuck it out.

Non-Christians in the group

If the group is open to the public, there may be non-Christians in the group. Most participants respect the Christian nature of the group and perhaps may learn more about God from it. God may even use the bereavement to gain the attention of someone who has been seeking a personal faith.

Social events - potlucks, parties

As the group continues to bond and recover, they will begin to take an interest in some social activities. They should be encouraged to call one another, perhaps have coffee together or meet for dinner before the group time. A potluck supper the week following the end of the class series can be good idea. If the group has bonded well, they usually want to continue meeting socially. They may meet either with or without the leader; if the group shares some of the responsibility for the events, it will help them in starting their new social life.

Completion and moving forward

Each group has its own personality and dynamics and there are as many levels of recovery as there are individuals. There are several options for a group which has completed the 10-week class. Some members are ready to move out into the world on their own and will leave the group. Some need to repeat the class material. Some may be able to assist with subsequent groups or even start their own group as a facilitator in another church. It is always helpful to have someone who can substitute when the leader is unable to attend the group. It is also possible to form a covenant group from the membership to continue meeting on a regular basis for fellowship, Bible study, and support.

For those who have reached a good level of recovery fairly quickly but still want to continue in a class together, an advanced 10-week session can be helpful. For this reason, I developed another workbook, *The Next Step: Moving On*, which deals more in depth with starting a new life. This class has been very successful in helping recovering widows and widowers find new purpose for their lives.

Surviving Christmas and the Holidays

As Thanksgiving and Christmas approach, bereaved persons may start to experience a high level of anxiety. The pressures of getting through the preparations for the holidays may begin to show in increased sadness Some group members may report a return to former levels of grief; others may feel that they just can't get through the holidays alone.

Starting to talk about the holidays as early as the first of November can help prepare the group for the coming months. It is important for group members to be able to express their fears and anxiety. The problem seems to be twofold: first, the fear that memories of past holidays will sweep over them and engulf them in renewed pain at the remembered loss, and, secondly, the fear that they will not be able to function with their families at the same level as before.

Widows and widowers need to be reassured that their fears are normal and that by recognizing them they can begin to overcome them. Some will want to travel to visit family or friends, thereby escaping the holidays at home. Others will welcome some group activity that will fill the empty spaces. They need to be told that they don't need to do as much as in the past; that they can relax and start creating new patterns and traditions. The supplemental material in the workbook on how to survive the holidays can be helpful as an aid to discussion.

Other grief support resources

The leader may find that some of the bereaved who come to the group need professional care, especially if there are deep psychological wounds or problems which have not been healed or resolved in the past. In this case, the bereavement will tend to intensify the problems. It must be made very clear at the beginning of the series that the leader is not a professional counselor.

There are sometimes local professionally led grief support groups available with regard to other losses, such as children and parents. These can usually be found through city Social Services Departments or counselors in private practice.

Resulting Objective:

To help widowers and widows remember the past without pain and to become whole persons again.

In Conclusion:

It is extremely gratifying to see the progress that group members make in even 10 weeks. The simple step of coming to the first class can make all the difference. If they continue through the series, it is exciting to see the changes in their lives. In the several decades that we have had widows and widowers grief recovery groups at Menlo Park Presbyterian Church and in the East Bay of San Francisco, thousands of people have walked through our doors and left refreshed in spirit. Some have made new commitments to the Lord and others have had a new door to faith opened to them. Not all have accepted our faith, but none have gone away untouched. It has always been interesting, exciting, and amazing to see what the Lord does each meeting night!

GRIEF RECOVERY

Bibliography and Suggested Reading

Although there are many excellent books on grief, I found two to be exceptionally helpful in understanding the grieving process and taking practical steps to recovery: Seven Choices by Elizabeth Harper Neeld, PhD., and The Grief Recovery Handbook by John W. James and Frank Cherry.

Most public libraries and book stores have extensive literature on grief recovery. Christian book stores also have a good selection on grieving as well as single life.

Bibliography

Seven Choices. Elizabeth Harper Neeld, PhD. Clarkson N. Potter Inc./Publishers. Distributed by Crown Publishers, Inc. New York, 1990.
A personally applied approach to the grieving process based on the premise that we must make choices in order to recover.

There is a new and updated version available in paperback:
Seven Choices: Finding Daylight after Loss Shatters Your World, 2003.

The Grief Recovery Handbook. John W. James and Frank Cherry. Harper and Row, 1988. Practical emphasis on processing through grief and dealing with past losses through study of a personal Loss History Graph.

This book has been reissued as **The Grief Recovery Handbook, 20th Anniversary Expanded Edition**. John W. James and Russell Friedman. William Morrow. 2017

On Death and Dying: *What the dying have to teach doctors, nurses, clergy and their own families.* Elisabeth Kübler-Ross. Macmillan, NY 1969
The research of Kübler-Ross is the basis of much of what we know about the grieving process before the death of a loved one.

The Courage to Grieve. Judy Tatlebaum. Harper &Row 1980, Lippincott& Crowell 2008. Good, positive self-help book offering specific techniques for grief work and resolution.

Understanding Grief, A Guide for the Bereaved. Howard J. Lunche. HowardLunche.com. 1997 and 2020

52 Simple Ways to Make Christmas Special. Jan Dargatz, Oliver Nelson, Publishers

GRIEF RECOVERY

Suggested Reading

Getting to the Other Side of Grief: Overcoming the Loss of a Spouse. Susan J. Zonnebelt-Smeenge and Robert C. De Vries. Second Edition. BakerBooks 2019

Good Grief. Granger E. Westberg. Fortress Press, Minneapolis. Original Edition copyright 1962. Updated and expanded Edition 2019

It's OK that you're Not OK: Meeting Grief and Loss in a Culture That Doesn't Understand. Megan Devine, Sounds True Incorporated, 2017

Second firsts: Live, Laugh, and Love Again. Christina Rasmussen, Hay House, 2013

Tear Soup: A recipe for Healing after Loss. Pat Schwiebert and Chuck DeKlyen, Grief Watch, Portland, OR. This is written by a hospice nurse with years of experience helping people on their grief journeys.

The Heart's Journey. Judy Pelikan, Abbeville Press Publishers (Tiny book that is good to use as a gift to a grieving person.)

The Other Side of Sadness: What the New Science of Bereavement Tells Us About Life After Loss." George A. Bonanno, Perseus Basic Books, 2009

GRIEF RECOVERY

Other Books
by
Robyn Ledwith Mar

How to Recover from Loss
Understanding and Recovering from Grief
(Other Losses)
Published 2011
Available at Amazon.com

A Time to Grieve
A Christian Guide to Comforting and Counseling
Those who are Grieving
Published 2013
Available at Amazon.com

Grief Recovery
The Next Step: Moving On
A Workbook for Recovering Widows and Widowers
Published 2015
Available at Amazon.com

GRIEF RECOVERY

Notes and Journaling

GRIEF RECOVERY

Notes and Journaling

GRIEF RECOVERY

Notes and Journaling

GRIEF RECOVERY

Notes and Journaling

GRIEF RECOVERY

Notes and Journaling

GRIEF RECOVERY

Notes and Journaling

Notes and Journaling

GRIEF RECOVERY

Notes and Journaling

GRIEF RECOVERY

Notes and Journaling

Printed in the United States
by Baker & Taylor Publisher Services